T0144070

THE HOOK UP

What you were never told about relationships

DR. EVON KIMBERLY

 www.trafford.com

North America & international
toll-free: 1 888 232 4444 (USA & Canada)
phone: 250 383 6864 ♦ fax: 812 355 4082

CONTENTS

DEDICATION

I would like to dedicate my first book to the memory of my grandparents Jesse & Earlee Rhodes and John & Hazel Smith.

I would like to give all honor and praises to my Savior Jesus Christ.

I would like to thank my parents, Charles and Zelma Smith,

My Family,

And my Church Family for all their love and support.

Also I would like to give an honorable mention to my special friend Starr, for helping me to see that a course correction was necessary in my life

Also I'd like to thank P. D. for catching me in my ocean.

CHAPTER 1
MOVING

WHENEVER I LOOK ON DATING sites, I'm always tickled by how many people say "I don't have baggage." The reality is that EVERYONE has baggage. The issue is where is your baggage? Still on the moving van or in your closet? I think that many relationships do not work out because folks get involved while in "movement" not after moving. When you move the first thing that you do is tell your landlord, friends, neighbors, post office and creditors. Second, you reserve a means for transporting your crap to the new location. Third, you clean up your mess in hopes of a return on your deposit. Fourth, you move out of your old place. Fifth, you unpack and re-establish yourself in new location. All of these things seem perfectly simple and normal. However, in terms of a relationship, this is much easier said than done. In regards to a relationship, the same rules apply. You are not moved until you have unpacked and re-established yourself somewhere else emotionally.

First, you tell everyone of the breakup. Second, you make emotional, mental, and sometimes physical accommodations for yourself to move on. Third, after you have accepted the life change, most people do what is necessary to clean up or make amends with their ex. Others will choose not to make amends and will forfeit the deposit on what was contributed into the relationship. Sometimes it is necessary to make a clean break if the situation is abusive or if both parties are unable to communicate. However, you should always be cautious of entering a relationship with a person who has unresolved issues with their ex. Finally the move . . . the relationship has ended and now you are somewhere else emotionally. However you still are in "movement" because you have not unpacked your memories, hurts, disappointments. Once you have unpacked and settled in some, it is time to announce your arrival. At this point you are officially moved.

The problem that many people face is that they move, unpack and then begin to think about the deposit that they left behind (AKA the ex) because they failed to clean up beforehand. So these are the folks who will run back to their ex trying to make amends or attempting to re-kindle. These people are still in movement and you should not enter into relationship with them. A person who is in movement is not stable emotionally and may disappoint you in a relationship so . . . beware! The fact that they may have a desire to correct past issues with an ex can be a healthy part of closure. However it can also be a sign that they are curious about the deposit left behind. Some people never finish moving because they never allow themselves time enough to unpack and settle in. These people live out of emotional suitcases. They jump from relationship to relationship without taking time to settle from their last movement.

How to determine stage of move

When you meet someone the first question that you should ask is how long has it been since your previous relationship? Now remember that some people move rather quickly, but it's the unpacking and curiosity about deposit that you should be concerned with. People will fool you and lead you to believing that they have moved and are settled emotionally. Do not ignore the signs! Usually if a person proclaims to have moved but is not settled or unpacked, you will see emotional boxes lying around. This means that they may often speak of their ex. They may seem detached or not completely available emotionally. They may show intense anger or sorrow in regards to their past situation. They may try to rush into making things serious between the two of you in order to mask true feelings. They may cheat to avoid and mask true feelings. They may engage in substance use (drugs/alcohol) and other reckless behaviors to mask true feelings.

If you meet someone and clearly they are moved but unpacking then understand that they may be on an emotional rollercoaster for a while. So if you choose to stay with a person in this situation you need to have a lot of patience. Some people will present like they have moved but in reality they are still renting space in another person's place which means they are too involved in previous situations. This means that they are too involved with their previous ex affairs. Sometimes people who are people pleasers will rent space after they have moved to preserve the feelings of another. Also some may be renting space in another place to protect their own personal interests, so be careful.

Now if a person is in fact moved, you will see the evidence of this in conversations and actions. They will be well adjusted to their new situation. They will own their mistakes and will not present to have hostility or anger towards previous relationships. High emotion and anger are signs of emotional suitcases that have not yet been unpacked . . . be careful! A person who is moved, unpacked and settled will be okay with past mistakes and will embrace where they are today. They will adequately have dealt with their move and you will see that they are happy, unique, whole and separated. They are healthy and this is a winner so grab em!!!

CHAPTER 2
UNDERSTANDING WORK RELATIONSHIPS

MY FIRST JOB WAS AT a Mexican fast food restaurant. Initially I worked as a cashier and then I was trained to do all functions of the job including food prep, clean up, and drive thru window. I remember having a supervisor who made life hell. This woman was on a serious power trip and I remember pondering why a middle aged woman would be exploiting power when the job is in fast food. This isn't Wall Street! She taught me my very first lesson in the work force.

Lesson number one is when a middle-age person is working on a job that only pays minimum wages and they don't own or manage the joint then that can spell trouble. I have learned that many of these types are in these jobs out of necessity and they hate the smell of youthfulness. The best thing to do on your job is to just keep your attitude and anger under control. Sometimes you will feel cursed by having a horrible supervisor. Perhaps your boss criticizes too much, is lazy, or micro manages. Believe it or not these types of experiences help you to learn how to manage personalities better. The lesson that I learned here was that it is important to understand what other people are going through. Sometimes, that supervisor is so mean because she was abused growing up and relate to people in the manner in which she was treated. Perhaps she does not have any control in any other area of her life and this is why she power trips. You can endure difficult situations a lot better when you learn to develop patience for other people and what they may be going through. You may not actually care what your supervisor is going through but if you act like you do, you will probably have an easier time at work. Everyone wants to be understood

Lesson number two was learned when I worked at an Amusement Park. My supervisor was an African American lady that wore a red jacket with a matching red visor every day at work. I did not believe that my supervisor liked other people of color. As an African American woman myself, I was prepared for racist people in the job force but never imagined that I'd have to battle it out among one of my own. I remember being promoted to Assistant Lead. I really should have been the Lead but the job was given to my lazy co-worker instead. The promotion for my co-worker was a blatant slap in my face because I was more qualified for the job but I accepted the Assistant position because it was more money. I eventually quit the job because I went toe to toe with my supervisor and I did not appreciate how she spoke to me. She was often putting me down and speaking in a loud obnoxious tone. I noticed that she only spoke with me in this way when my co-workers were present. The lesson learned here is do not assume that you are safe because you are among your own ethnicity. Also when you are unhappy on your job and are being treated badly, it's best to develop an exit plan. I quit the job abruptly and the lack of funds hurt me in the end. I learned that I should have been looking for another job prior to the blow out.

Lesson number three was learned at a hardware store. I learned that if you really want a job and you are persistent, you can get it. The first time I applied at the hardware store I did not get a response or even an interview. I really wanted this job because it paid $5.00 per hour and minimum wage was 4.25 at the time. The second time I applied at the hardware store, I did not get a response and so I went into the store to follow up on my application. I met the manager and he told me that they had not started the interview process yet and to be patient. I kept coming back to visit my old friend and kept inquiring about my application. I must have gone into that store four times to speak with the manager. On that last trip I guess he got tired of seeing me and said we will be doing interviews tomorrow and invited me to come back. I happily agreed to return for a 1pm interview and was hired on the spot. Lesson learned here is that persistence, when you allow people to become familiar with you through persistence, often will have a break through.

Lesson number 4 was learned at a Foster Family Agency. The lesson is stand for something or you lie down for everything and also be careful what you wish for. I had a supervisor that was a racist and during the staff meetings she would refer to people of color as "those people". She was not even discrete about her racist comments. I remember sitting in her office and confronting her on the comments made during our staff meeting. I remember her actually admitting to me that her parents were racist and that she had tried hard not to absorb their ways. I reported my concerns to the Manager but because he was personal friends with the Supervisor he disregarded my grievances. Although I really needed the job I just could not work for an agency that had such disrespect for people of color when I am one. I always was taught that if someone would speak in a derogatory manner about an ethnic group then they will speak about me in that same way when I am not around. However, I'm sure that this woman would have spoken her mind in front of me. I just had to stand up for myself and resign from the position. I remember going to the supervisor's office and speaking to her privately about my desire to quit my job. She called me ungrateful and said that other "black little girls" would be happy to have this job. I only remember seeing red and then out of my Christian mouth came "I hope something crawls up your @#$! And dies!" Some years later I learned that she had anal cancer and died. The lesson that I learned here, besides be careful what you wish for, is that it's important to stand up for what you believe. My integrity cannot be bought.

Lesson five was learned at multiple jobs. It is important to always write down what you did each day on a calendar and print out all concerning emails for your own records. On many of my jobs from the past my whereabouts or work habits were brought into question. First let me clarify that I am a very consciencious worker. However, sometimes people want you to fail and you must be prepared to protect yourself. I have progressed in my career because everyone knows that I document, document, document. When people know that you are careful and that you keep evidence that you are doing your job it becomes more difficult for them to create pitfalls. The lesson that I learned is that although you may have good intentions everyone doesn't always see your intentions and it is best to keep good records.

Lesson six I learned at a social service job. Sometimes your success on a job is determined by how well you fit in with the culture of the workplace. It does not matter if you do a great job what matters on some jobs is whether or not you fit in the "club." Remember that it is not worth having membership in some clubs. It is okay to decide to quit a job if the culture is not for you. If you do not fit in, personnel will not hesitate to fire you. Why not fire them first if you know you don't fit in. I learned that people can and will fire you from a job simply for not fitting in.

I learned lesson seven at a small business. If you work for a company that has proven itself to operate unprofessionally then don't be surprised when you get treated unfairly or in an unprofessional manner. Don't think that certain treatment is isolated to certain instances or people. If the owner or manager is "ghetto" then the entire operation is "ghetto."

Lesson eight I had to learn the hard way. The lesson is that there are NO FRIENDS on your job! Now the exception to this rule would be if you knew a person before you became employed together. Having "friends" on my job has created nothing but problems. Also have absolutely NO RELATIONSHIPS on your job. The issue with having friends on the job is that you really want to confide in them about the frustrations of management, supervisors, work conditions, etc. It really doesn't seem like a problem sharing these things at the time until something you said gets leaked or better yet one of your "friends" gets promoted. Now that your friend is a boss they really aren't much your friend anymore because there is a code where bosses and employees should not fraternize. Soon you are being treated differently by management and you don't understand why. You talk too much, that's why! It should be obvious to anyone with a brain that having romantic relationships on your job is not a wise choice. For a small percentage, it will end in marriage and hooray for you. However, for most of us the relationship will end tragically and now you will have a stalker on your job. You may find yourself stuck because you will not feel comfortable telling an employer that this person that you once dated is now stalking and harassing you when there is clearly a rule in the employee manual which states no dating co-workers.

Lesson nine is know your rights as an employee. Many people do not realize that there are people who can help you advocate for your employee rights such as Fair Housing and Employment and Union Representatives. It is important to know that if you are accused of doing something wrong on your job or you feel mistreated you do not have to meet with your supervisor or sign anything without consulting with an attorney or union representative first. Also you can ask your union representative to be present at all meetings if you feel like you need a witness or support. People who know their personal rights do prevail.

Lesson ten is that during staff parties, luncheons, and events, you are still at work. I know that it seems safe to drink alcohol and let down your hair because after all, this is on your time but you are not safe. You are still at work at any work function so be on your best behavior. Also do not bring people to the event that may offend or flirt with co-workers. This may affect your relationships with others at work.

CHAPTER 3
LOVE HANGOVER

Do you wear your wedding ring on the wrong finger because you married the wrong person? Before we can explore why people are marrying the wrong partners we must look to those who married the right persons for guidance. I interviewed couples who had been married for 10+ years on why they thought marriages were failing today.

Couple #1: An elderly lady married for 56 years once told me that "in love" does not refer to the feelings that you have for another. She said that "in love" refers to the inner feelings that you have for yourself while in relationship with another. She said that if you feel encouraged, motivated, inspired, and free then you are indeed "in love." She said that our younger generation is confused about what real love means.

Couple #2: The wife stated that marriage is not seen the same as it was years ago. The husband shared that when he and his wife got married they had nothing. He explained that they built everything together. He stated that they operated as a team. He stated that his wife did all the budgeting and he trusted her completely. He said that these days couples don't seem to work together or to allow their partners to complement them. Everyone is so busy protecting their own interests and no one is working together.

Couple #3: The wife stated that if she would have known how much work marriage involved, then she would not have married her husband. She shared that there was a time for an entire year when she wanted him to leave but he refused to go. Today they are happily married and she is glad that he didn't leave.

Couple 4: One gentleman said, "This is a microwave generation and everyone wants their way right now. Marriage does not always work in your favor immediately. Sometimes it may take a year or two to get over a rough patch but when you are committed to staying, you work it out eventually."

Couple #5: A wife stated that marriages don't last today because people are not seeing their spouse as family. She explained how she matured into a different person from whom her husband had married. "Change and growth are a part of marriage." She stated that sometimes your spouse may grow into someone that you love and sometimes they may grow into someone that you don't like but you must learn to accept that. She stated, "family doesn't abandon family".

Is marriage not taken seriously?

I think that the divorce rate is so high because there is no exit clause in marriage. If you join a gym membership, sign up for a new cell phone service or even take a job there is always an exit clause or a loop hole to get you out of your commitment without stiff penalty. Let's face it, society has changed and no one wants to feel stuck with a lemon nor make lemonade anymore. Perhaps our marriage laws should change to accommodate a changing society. What if a marriage license was designed to expire. What if we could choose to renew our marriage license every so many years instead of signing on for a lifetime? What if you had to demonstrate that you knew what it took to successfully maintain your marriage? What if certain indiscretions during the marriage could result in your marriage license or your privilege to get married being suspended or terminated? What if certain indiscretions required you to go to marriage school in order to keep your license in good standing? What if you were required to carry marriage insurance to cover incidentals such as the cost of marriage school or emotional damages? Imagine if people had to take and pay for a marriage education course, marriage application training and take a test prior to marrying. Would this be enough to discourage someone who is impulsive or who really doesn't want to work hard in a marriage? Is hard work the issue?

Marrying type

Clearly times have changed and so have value systems. How does one identify a person who is going to stick in there with them for life? Well, my grandmother always said that you will know a tree by its fruits. This basically means that you need to see if the person is able to commit in other areas of their life. People will make decisions but there is a difference between making a decision and making a strong commitment.

Perhaps you should look at the history of long term commitments in their life. How often does the person make decisions and not follow through? Wouldn't it be nice if people came with something similar to credit scores but in regards to their commitment history? Then you could simply look at their scores and know their history of commitment and follow through on important past decisions. However, there is no such tool so you just have to ask the right questions and use common sense.

While I was in my mid-twenties I was engaged to be married and I am really happy that we didn't follow through on that. In my forties I have realized that my mentality back then was not conducive to marriage. For example, I refused to purchase or lease thinking that I may want to move out of the State or Country. I kept with that logic for many years and clearly I was not leaving the state of California but I used that as an excuse to not commit. I would not commit to any long term memberships. I enjoyed living month to month and having the option to break the agreement whenever I desired. I changed jobs often and changed friends/relationships often. The only long term commitment that I had was my car note and honestly I did not consistently pay it on time monthly. These should be seen as red flags for anyone looking to marry. If you do not see many commitment fruits, then that person may not be a good candidate for marriage.

Married to Family

Also I agree with couple #5 in that, once you marry, your spouse should be seen as your family. I think this is the major reason why the divorce rate is so high. There is no sense of family anymore. People change over the years, whether you are married or not. My parents are completely different from who they were when I was growing up. Sometimes, you may grow to love a whole different person from whom you married. Sometimes you may grow to dislike or grow apart in interests from the person you married. Growing is a major part of marriage and life. Many people accept the changes and hang in there. I definitely do not suggest remaining in a relationship that is abusive or harmful. The reason why the divorce rate is so high is because the meaning of family has changed within our society.

I cannot get rid of a close family member because they have grown into someone that I do not like. I will simply cope and tolerate the change in the best way I can. I may disagree on some things with my brother but I do not get to walk away from the relationship or switch him out for another brother when I think things aren't working out. I learn to cope with the changes, disagreements and disappointments because he is my family and that is what family does.

Maybe people should be asking, "will you family me?" instead of "will you marry me?" Before you get married ask yourself if you love your partner enough to stay married now for who they are and later for who they may become even if you don't like who that is. Some might say, don't I have a right to be happy? My response to that question is . . . Absolutely! However, happiness is what you create it to be so focus on what is good.

CHAPTER 4
HUNGRY

WHY DO WE CHOOSE THE wrong people over and over again? Most times we pick the wrong people because we are hungry. Have you ever gone to a grocery store when you were hungry? You tend to pick fast foods which are satisfying for the time being but not as fulfilling as a whole meal. You pick the wrong people because you are making hungry choices out of your hungry needs. According to my Pastor, if you are hungry and desperate, you will make poor unsatisfying choices . . . hungry choices. The horrible part about it is the choice usually will not seem like a poor choice immediately. You will settle in with the person but soon you will realize that they do not fulfill you . . . they were just a snack.

How to make better choices

Now at some time or another we all are hungry so how do we avoid making hunger choices? The key to the problem here is simple. You pretend that you are full and choose as if you are full even when you are not. This is what will bring you the best results. If you are tired of being a snacker then hold out for the seven course meal. The first thing that you have to do is recognize when you are hungry. Making hungry choices is a habit and can be broken. Once you are recognizing that you have a need the next step is identifying what the need is. Do you want sex? Do you need to be held? Do you just need a little companionship? Once you know the need you are on your way.

You will have to spend some time with yourself thinking about if you were to order your seven course meal what you would want it to be. Now keep in mind while you are developing your menu, Reeses Peanut butter Cups are going to look very appealing because you are hungry but deny yourself and pretend you are full. If you deprive your stomach of food, it will shrink, causing your stomach to require less food. Deprivation will also cause your hungry need to shrink, causing you to require less foolishness. Now what is going to bring you the most satisfaction? Write it down if necessary. What would an amazing person be like for you characteristic-wise? Remember you are looking for amazing characteristics, not amazing possessions. Now that you know what you want from the menu, it is time to put out invitations for amazing.

Socialize and do whatever you were doing to meet people and maybe try some new locations. Begin to interview people for having the amazing qualities that you have developed on your menu. Now it is true that no one is perfect, but we are not looking for perfect, we are looking for amazing for you. Do not lower your standards and hold true to your desires. Don't be afraid of rejecting people because really you are saving them and yourself a great deal of wasted time.

Once you meet your seven-course meal don't run to the table. If you run to the table you may scare the person off. Also if you present as desperate, this may be perceived as unattractive. Take your time and get familiar with the person. Remember you are not going to behave as though you are hungry. Do not rush into sex. Take your time and savor one taste at a time. Take it in slowly. Don't eat too fast. If you eat too fast you can end up with indigestion or worse. Moving too fast can ruin a beautiful possibility. Let their background, experiences, values digest slowly with you. Take the time to see if what they are offering is going to be long term satisfying. Now understand that this may not be Mr. or Miss Right but at least the meal will be much more enjoyable. Also you will not be hungry again for a while.

CHAPTER 5
LOOPY

BEFORE YOU CAN HAVE GOOD and healthy relationships, you must know yourself, and how you relate to the world around you. The most important relationship that you can have is the one with yourself. If I could go back in a time machine and meet up with my 16-year-old self I would tell her to follow through with her promises to herself. It's funny but we don't think much about breaking promises to ourselves. It could be something as simple as saying to yourself "I'm going to go to the gym four days a week" and then not doing it.

When you set a goal and tell yourself that you are going to do something and then not follow through it becomes a deduction out of your bank of confidence account. It's one thing to lie to others, but when you lie to yourself, a huge deduction comes out of your account. At the time it doesn't feel like a deduction in fact you may rather enjoy what you did instead of following through with your word. However, each time that you break your word to yourself there is a deduction with extra fees. Some people lie to themselves so much that they are overdrawn. The only unfortunate thing is that you are not going to get a little note in the mail informing you of your overdraft. Eventually you will begin to stop setting goals at all because you no longer have the confidence to be optimistic.

I would also tell my young self that there is not a loophole in everything. In life there are no short cuts when it comes to relationships. I was the master of loopholes. If there was a loophole to be found I discovered it. At a very young age I learned that I did not want to work hard. When you are young, having this position is difficult without appearing to be lazy. When I was young, I lacked wisdom but I still did not want to work hard so I guess that did make me a bit lazy. I never considered myself to be the brightest bulb on the tree but certainly not the dimmest.

I did not know how to grow out of my laziness. I figured out a way to get out of doing work and to manipulate others into doing it for me most of the time. The funny part is that I often did get over therefore there was not anything encouraging me to not be lazy. I managed to manipulate my situations enough to bring positive results most times. During the times that I did receive unfavorable results I chalked it up to bad luck that day.

It's one thing to think that you are not the brightest but another thing for someone else to say this. I remember my high school teacher saying that I would never be able to attend college because my grades weren't high enough and I simply lacked motivation. I remember a fear falling over me after she made that statement. I had attended private college preparatory schools since first grade. Did my parent's waste money on an over-priced education and their kid just wasn't smart enough to make the cut? Many would say that what the teacher said to me was a horrible thing but I don't anymore. This statement created a dialogue in my head that never had occurred before. I began to wonder if I really was not smart enough to make it in college. I found myself in despair although I really was not looking forward to doing hard work in college anyhow. It was the thought that someone had told me that I would not make the cut. Where was the loophole in this?

At this point in my young life I had created so many loop holes, I had no idea of what I was really capable of. I had made so many promises to myself but I never followed through completely because I found a loop hole. My account was bankrupt. I did not have the confidence to apply myself because although finding loopholes was fun, indirectly I was telling myself that I was not capable of completing a task. One day I spoke with my school counselor about my situation and he shared some words of wisdom that changed my life. He said two things: "you can never let others' opinions of you create your reality" and "where you are today is no reflection on where you can be in your future." Some folks might say *find yourself*, but I would say *create yourself*. I liked the thought of not working hard but creating is work.

My father worked as a janitor most of my childhood. He showed me his calloused hands and told me that my hands should never look like his. He said that in life there are those that use their brain and those that use their hands. He said that I needed to learn how to use my brain. I respect my father because he is intelligent and definitely was not a lazy man. He worked very hard all the time. I watched my mother leave for work every morning at 5am to her office job. She always wore nice professional clothing. I remember thinking that I wanted to be a professional just like my mother. She also worked very hard. I wanted to be respected just like my parents.

I realized for the first time that respect is earned. It is a horrible thing when you are not sure of your own potential or capabilities. It's even worse to avoid struggle due to laziness. Progress can never occur without struggle. Someone once told me that when you are on a plane you may experience turbulence when you change elevation. In life, struggle is our turbulence and elevation is our desired change. I would tell my young self that I am not on a permanent layover and to board the plane.

CHAPTER 6
CHEATERS LAW

I HAVE BEEN ON BOTH sides of this coin. I have been a cheater and have also suspected that I was cheated on. Now it's funny to me that people tend to judge a cheater and pass judgment before knowing or understanding the situation. Is it ever okay to cheat? I think it is a matter of perspective which definitely should be explored. Usually this is the part when people accuse me of not holding a cheater accountable for their actions. For the record, I am not excusing anyone's poor choices and as an adult, I think everyone should be accountable for their own actions. However let's explore the cheater through a different lens and see if your prospective remains the same.

In the dictionary the definition of murder is the killing of another human being but there are conditions specifically outlined in the law describing the four different types of murder and each brings different sentencing options. This logic implies that even though a person is dead, motive should be included in determining the degree of wrongdoing. There is murder with premeditation or deliberation or occurring during the commission of another serious crime (first degree murder). Then there is murder without intent or premeditation (second degree murder). Voluntary Manslaughter is the unintentional act of accidentally killing of another through carelessness. Involuntary Manslaughter is killing someone without having intent to cause injury. First degree murder holds a more serious sentencing because of intent while involuntary manslaughter holds a less serious sentence. Now suppose we used this same type of logic as it applies to cheating.

First degree cheating would be a person who thought about cheating, planned to cheat, identified a person to cheat with, and formulated a plan to avoid being caught cheating. Also if a person commits an additional offense against the relationship while cheating, such as cheating with the partner's friend or relative this is considered first degree cheating.

Second degree cheating would be someone who did not intend or plan to cheat but did. This person cheated with someone with whom they had a previous romantic history or interest. They got caught up into a moment. They also could have had judgment clouded due to substance use. This person has a previous history of cheating/dishonesty.

Voluntary Sex slaughter is when a person had been suffering from emotional and or physical neglect in the relationship. This person wants to remain in the relationship. This person did not intend on cheating but one day they allowed someone to fill a lonely void and sex was the result. This sex act was not planned or intentional. This person may also be dealing with a partner who has a history of cheating or who is abusive. This person does not have a previous history of cheating.

Involuntary Sex slaughter is when a person thought the relationship was over while still in it. The person may even have expressed and discussed the rocky relationship with current partner. This person is physically in a relationship but emotionally somewhere else and both parties know this. This person is most likely not sleeping with the partner but on the couch. The chemistry is gone from the relationship but this person is staying for reasons other than the maintenance of relationship. This person had sex with another and hurt the feelings of the current partner.

It's interesting how intent seems to make a difference with murder but not cheating. It is your choice whether or not you are going to stay with a person who cheated on you. However,

I do not think that all cheaters are created the same. I have heard the saying "once a cheater ... always a cheater." If you are struggling with the decision of whether or not to forgive or take back a person who has cheated, I think that you should consider the entire situation not just the act.

It's also important to remember that all people are vulnerable sometimes. A person once told me, "Men are as faithful as their options." I do not think this is a fair statement and it does not represent truth for all men. My auntie always says that "flesh is flesh and it doesn't matter whose bones it is on." That basically means that we are all tempted and vulnerable sometimes. Personally, I would take a risk with someone who cheated if their intent was not malicious (Voluntary and Involuntary Sex Slaughter). We as a society can become so judgmental, but I think we can all take a little time to examine ourselves for the last time we made a mistake out of our own insecurities, carelessness, and/or selfishness ... and let those without sin cast the first stone.

CHAPTER 7

.... WHERE'S MY GUN??

So you have met someone very special and now you are excited and falling in love. The sex is fantastic and you are wondering how you ever lived without the other. You are in the "where have you been all my life" place or what I'd like to call loading the bullet. It is fun but you must remember that you are only in stage one of relationship building . . . you have far to go. During this stage you are simply getting acquainted. You are becoming familiar with habits, hobbies, commitments, and values. You are loading the bullet and beginning the relationship process. During this stage many people "drop the bullet or load incorrectly." This means that during the learning process something has happened that was a huge turn off. During the first 0-12 weeks (3 months) it is socially acceptable to walk away, if things aren't working out. This may be hurtful but fair because commitment has not entered the picture.

The second stage of relationship begins at week 13 and ends at week 28 (6 months). I call this stage locking the chamber. During this stage you will begin to expand on your interests together by participating in mutually enjoyable outings but now you are inclusive of your friends. You are becoming more comfortable with each other. This should be securing and firming up what you have been developing so far. You are now learning how the person interacts with others that are close with you. You are also learning how your friends are interacting with your special person. You are assessing whether or not this person is going to fit into your personal social circle. You are becoming known as a couple.

Now that the gun is loaded and the chamber is locked, you need to remove the safety. This will usually occur beginning in week 29 and may continue through week 40 (9 month) or longer. At this time, you have expanded and introduced the person to family or closer friends. You have gone on vacation or short day trip together. You are beginning to think about long term goals with this person. You are the most vulnerable during this stage because you are opening up and putting your guards/safety down. You want the person to see you for who you are and accept you. It is important to understand that this stage takes the longest for most people. Often times, folks are in this stage for years depending on levels of security. Now if you have completed this stage successfully with your significant other it is time to aim the gun.

Aiming the gun means that you feel secure in what you have and you know that you want this relationship and you have a target in mind. Perhaps your goal is marriage, moving in together or something else but you are now aiming at a very specific target. To aim and shoot the gun means that you have gone through all the needed steps and you feel secure enough to ask that person to aim and shoot for the target with you. Shooting the gun is a task accomplished together.

If you have been in a relationship for less than 4 months then you have barely even loaded the gun. To tell someone that you are in love or catching feelings within the first 3 months might be a little premature. Be careful! This may scare your love interest off. Also if you sharing a great deal of time with your love interest it may feel like you have known him or her for years but remain focused on the facts and the actual amount of time you have been together. Now during the locking of the chamber stage is when a lot of couples fall off the radar. Often times integrating friends can be a complicating factor. Many people seek the approval of their close friends and therefore if they do not fit into one's personal social circle it can be disastrous. Breaking up during the safety stage is always very hurtful because you are hoping to gain complete acceptance from the other.

How long does it take to load and shoot a gun? Each couple is very different but in most healthy scenarios it takes at least 9 months or longer to load and shoot. If it takes 9 months to develop a human life, why should we believe that it would take less than that to combine two lives?

CHAPTER 8
GETTING TO KNOW YOU QUESTIONS

The Questions you should be asking

- How long has it been since your last relationship?
- Have you ever been abused in a relationship? Have you ever hit or abused?
- Have you ever been married? Common Law Married? Domestic Partnership?
- Have you ever been accused of or arrested for stalking?
- Have you ever had any restraining orders?
- Have you ever gone to jail behind a relationship?
- Describe your work history? How long on each job?
- Do you have a criminal history?
- Have you ever been hospitalized for medical or mental health issues?
- Do you take any medications?
- Do you have any health issues?
- Have you had any surgeries?
- Have you ever destroyed someone else's property?
- Have you ever been in a cult? Do you serve a dark power?
- Do you have children? Did you ever have children? How many alive and dead?
- Have you ever had CPS involvement in your life? Why?
- Have you ever been abused as a child?
- Have you ever been raped?
- Have you ever had an STD?
- When was last time you had AIDS test?
- Have you ever had an abortion?
- Have you ever killed?
- Have you ever stolen?
- As a child did you ever stay at any juvenile detention centers?
- How is your credit?

- Do you pay your bills on time?
- Do you have a good relationship with your family?
- Do you family/friends know about your lifestyle?
- Have you ever used any drugs?
- Do you smoke anything?
- Do you own a gun? If so, have you fired it?
- Is there a possibility that someone in your family may have to come live with you in future?
- Have you ever had ANY sexual contact with same sex?
- Have you ever cheated?
- Do you have any regrets from past relationships?
- Have you been baptized? Do you believe in God?
- Are you a member of any clubs or organizations?
- Have you ever started a fire which required intervention?
- Have other people ever said you had a problem with gambling, drugs, drinking, sex, porn?
- Have you ever had sex with someone who was forbidden (ex: friend's partner, relative, under aged person)
- Considering all that is going on in the world around you, what grieves your heart the most? What brings you the most pleasure?
- If you could change something about yourself, what would it be & why?
- When did you last have the heartiest laugh?
- Tell me about a favorite event of your adulthood/childhood. Saddest event?
- Do you consider yourself OCD, very clean, tidy, messy, a slob?
- Have you ever participated in any form of diversion classes?
- Have you ever changed your name?
- Do you have medical/dental insurance?

- Do you have a 401K?
- Do you own property?
- What would your last partner say is the reason why you two broke up?
- Have you ever been homeless?
- Have you ever filed for bankruptcy?
- Have you ever co-signed for someone and had the deal go bad?
- Are you debt free? If not, why are you in debt?
- How many jobs have you had in last ten years?
- Who has the most influence in your life?
- Who do you seek approval from?
- Do you have any concerns about previous exs?
- Have you ever been to jail or prison?
- Have you ever gotten a DUI/DWI?
- Have you ever been in a physical altercation as an adult?
- Are you allergic to anything?
- What are the three most important things in your life?
- How many times have you been drunk/ high in last 7 days?
- Have you ever been charged with child endangerment/ child abuse/child molestation?
- Have you ever been charged with rape?
- Did your parents raise you? Were you adopted?
- Who pays your bills?
- Has anyone ever accused you of being controlling? If so, why?

CHAPTER 9

MAKING THE SALE
OR NOT

I LEARNED EVERYTHING THAT I ever needed to know about letting go and detaching from relationships from working in car sales.

Years ago, I worked as a car salesperson for Ford Motor Company. It was one of the most cut throat industries that I have ever worked in but I learned a lot. When a customer approached the lot you as a salesperson had to assert yourself by yelling "up." This indicated to all the other salespersons that this was your customer. Now sometimes there was debate about who called the "up" first but only the most assertive and aggressive would plow their way to the customer first. Now if for some reason the customer was not impressed with your sales pitch or showed signs that they were about to leave the lot, we were taught to turn the customer over to another salesperson asap.

Sometimes people have personal preferences such as preferring to work with men or simply wanting someone older and more experienced. A customer usually will not say what they are thinking and instead will abandon the situation by walking away from the car lot. The logic of turning to another salesperson was simply that it's better to have 50% of something then 100% of nothing. The customer receives the desired service and the goal of making the sale is met. Later the two sales persons would split the profit. Although we were competing against each other it was better to make the sale with teamwork than to lose the sale as an individual.

The lessons learned from this experience have helped me have a better understanding of relationships. You have to know how to identify a good opportunity for yourself (prospective sale). You have to be really honest with yourself (I'm going to lose this sale). You have to know when to let a person leave your life (turning to another salesperson). You have to know when to walk away. You have to know the value of the relationship and the impact of its loss (50% of something or 100% of nothing). You have to know how to preserve what is good.

Occasionally folks would walk onto the lot with absolutely no intensions of buying. Despite my efforts they were never going to purchase a car. Often times they had no means to buy and were just lookie Lous. Sometimes in life people are not ready to invest and you have to be able to see that this is not a good opportunity for a relationship. There will be times when a person may initially demonstrate that they were willing and ready to invest but when you run the credit scores you may learn differently. This is why it is important to take time to get to know a person long enough to discover truth.

Sometimes a person will be willing and ready to invest but later in life they lose interest and no longer do what is necessary to maintain the relationship. In car sales, we call this repossession. Don't be afraid to repo a relationship that has gone bad. People tend to stay in empty friendships/relationships that do not offer anything because they are holding on to the memory of what once was. The car industry doesn't care how many memories were shared. If you cannot contribute then the relationship is over. Why are we so patient in relationships that are not contributing a thing to us? Occasionally you must be honest with yourself and ask what is this relationship doing for me? Are you being over productive in the relationship? Are you the only one working to save the sale?

You see in car sales if I didn't have another salesperson to turn to, the sale would be lost. Relationship is the same as teamwork. If you don't have anyone to turn to and depend on, the sale (relationship) is lost. You only gain if both people are working together. Otherwise you are getting 100% of nothing. If you are in fact holding on to 100% of nothing then I highly recommend that you learn how to walk away. A relationship that brings you nothing 100% of the time also will drain you 100% of the time. My tip for walking away is simple. Everything dies when you don't feed it. If you stop feeding into a bad relationship it will die. This means stop calling, stop texting, stop making excuses, stop making time.

CHAPTER 10
SEX VS. LOVE

THERE IS A MAJOR DIFFERENCE between sex and love and the two should not be confused. Sex is about pleasing the mind and body. Love is about preserving what is good holistically. Often times, people think that they are in love but are not willing to do what is necessary to preserve what is good! This is not love! This is self seeking and old-fashioned selfishness and love isn't in it.

Be honest with yourself! If you just want fun, excitement, and sex there is nothing wrong with that. However, don't highjack people who are really looking for love and long term commitment to satisfy your own sexual needs. Hook up with those who are looking for the same thing that you are seeking. If you are looking for great sex let me tell you how to find it.

First of all there are four types of sex that you can have: bad, fair, good, and Dayuuum. I am going to skip the lessons on how to obtain the first three because I think it is important to concentrate on the latter. The following are the ten things you should know in order to find a compatible lover for the Dayuum affect.

1) Select someone who comes to the table with your same level of skill or better. I do not mind entertaining those with training wheels from time to time but not when I am looking for the Dayuuum effect. How do you know if a person has skill? You will never know for certain if a person has skill by just looking at them but you can make an educated guess. Some people just ooze sex appeal and others are just sexy. For example, in my opinion Prince oozes, Erik Bonet is sexy, Janet oozes and Beyonce is sexy. Personally, I would take a gamble on either type.

2) Now that you know that the person has some skill level your going to need them to match your level of adventure. You don't want someone who is apprehensive about doing certain things if you are uninhibited. You may need someone who would try anything no matter how kinky. The person also has to be uninhibited and this my friend is hard to find. Even the kinkiest person usually has some things that they will not try. Perhaps you would like to find that person who has tried the unimaginable and is looking for more. However, if you are inhibited in certain areas make sure that your partner share in those feelings. There is nothing worse than wanting something done to your body and your partner being unwilling to perform it.

3) Many can appreciate a dirty talker. It can be a turn on to hear how you have turned someone on and better yet how they plan on pleasing you. It lets you know that they are in control of your orgasm. However you do not want to trust everyone with this power. Although I can appreciate a dirty talker everyone does not want to hear your potty mouth. If a person seems turned off by your dirty talking outside of the bedroom then don't try it inside the bedroom. You will kill the moment.

4) Now that it is established that you are going to trust this person with your orgasm you must come to the main event with a plan. You should give some thought to what you want to do to the person prior to the main event and you may want to verbalize it in the nastiest kind of way.

5) It's important that you think about control. Do you like to drive, do you prefer that someone else drives or do

you like to switch drivers? The act can be complicated enough without power struggles and that can kill the moment. Before you hit the sack discuss the roles or establish an easy way to transition roles without struggle.

6) You need to be aware of what pleasures your MVP (most valuable P....) and your pleasure threshold (how long it takes you to orgasm). It is great to communicate this verbally or physically. There is nothing wrong with teaching someone how to please you. If a person takes offense to you communicating these things then scratch them off the list because they weren't going to bring good sex anyhow with that attitude. Stay in your lane! Don't try to engage in a three hour sex activity when you have a 15 minute pleasure threshold because you might get your ass kicked out of bed.

7) It's important to know if you like an easy touch or an aggressive/assertive lover. Whatever you like you better have that conversation before hitting the sack. I never appreciated the pillow prince/ss types. These types just lay there and there isn't much to be said about their performance but to each it's own. Nothing ruins the mood faster than a person not handling your MVP correctly. Surprisingly, older folks 40 and older are the animals in bed. Some people who are submissive outside of the bedroom are animals in bedroom because secretly they are into role play. TIP: If a submissive person is wearing sexy undies go for it!

8) Endurance/patience: A healthy person can endure hours of pleasuring. Sometimes it takes a while for a woman to climax and sometimes a woman enjoys climaxing over and over again .... Dayuum! A person

who is not in good shape will need to sleep immediately after orgasm. If you want to have Dayuum sex then you need a healthy person who can go the long haul. So hit the gym!!!

9) A person who isn't desperate but confident. This person isn't quick to jump into bed but is choosey. If there is anticipation and you have to work for it a bit the main event is intensified. If the sex comes too easily then it takes away from the fun. If you tease a bit, flirt a bit, your partner will explode like I shaken can soda. No one wants something that everyone can have. Many will not admit it but most love the chase.

10) Finally # 10 is Be IN TUNE and UNSELFISH. Take your time to explore the body and do those things that are pleasing in an unselfish way. To have a willingness to please your partner first is important. Having a connection or being in tune helps to intensify the event as well. The biggest orgasms come from what is done outside of the bedroom.

As I mentioned earlier there is a difference between having a romantic companion or FWB (friend with benefits) and love. First you must be honest with yourself about purpose. Many relationships have failed because one person is ready for love and the other is not. Sometimes you really want to be ready for a partnership and you really want to try because of what you feel for your significant other but you are just not ready. Everything goes back to being honest with oneself about purpose. Remember love is hard work and requires selflessness. If you're not ready, be honest with yourself and the person that you have highjacked.

Us Preserving Love

Being a life partner means that you trade in "Me and I" for "We and Us" just like in Michael Jackson's song "Ben". This applies to all areas of life (financial, spiritual, family, emotional, physical, etc). Sometimes people feel as if they are losing themselves when they trade in "Me and I" but if you feel this way then you probably aren't ready for a partnership. Trading in these words requires trust, faith, patience, understanding, and maturity. Imagine doing something life threatening with only your significant other standing nearby to aid you. In my case I think about jumping into the deep ocean blue because I can not swim. The thought of falling is scary enough but to voluntarily jump into the ocean? My significant other could be standing nearby, perhaps with a rescue hook or may even be an excellent swimmer but the fear still exists. Will this person let me drown or hurt myself? Will I have jumped to my doom? Love means that I am willing to take that dangerous jump and I trust that the other person will catch me because if they didn't it wouldn't be just the end of me but the end of "us." So the question is will the other person be capable of catching you in your most vulnerable moment? Are you capable of catching them? Do you trust that they would catch you if given the opportunity even if they are capable? Please remember that there is a difference between trying and doing. Either someone will be caught or not. Good intentions do not mean a hell of a lot if you are the one underneath the water.

I love the scene from the movie Titanic when they were out in the ocean and he finds a piece of furniture for her to climb on to stay a float. It was not large enough for them both but he placed her safety and survival above his own. Then there was the scene when he was trapped and handcuffed in the bottom deck of the ship. She risked her own life to free him to safety. I think that Titanic was such a powerful and romantic movie because it showed unselfish "us preserving" love. This is what I'd like to think true love is made of. Wouldn't we all like to meet a person that would love enough to not risk not losing "us?"

Printed in the United States
By Bookmasters